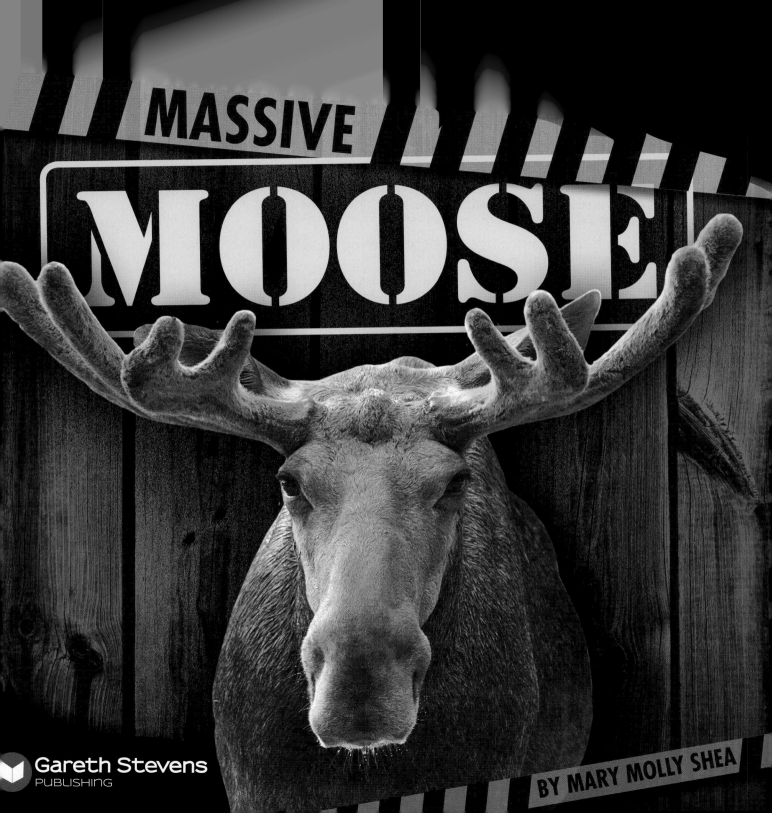

MASSIVE
MOOSE

BY MARY MOLLY SHEA

Gareth Stevens
PUBLISHING

Please visit our website, www.garethstevens.com. For a free color catalog of all our high-quality books, call toll free 1-800-542-2595 or fax 1-877-542-2596.

Library of Congress Cataloging-in-Publication Data

Names: Shea, Mary Molly, author.
Title: Massive moose / Mary Molly Shea.
Description: New York : Gareth Stevens Publishing, [2017] | Series: Cutest animals...that could kill you! | Includes bibliographical references and index.
Identifiers: LCCN 2016003172 | ISBN 9781482449198 (pbk.) | ISBN 9781482449136 (library bound) | ISBN 9781482449013 (6 pack)
Subjects: LCSH: Moose–Juvenile literature.
Classification: LCC QL737.U55 S524 2017 | DDC 599.65/7–dc23
LC record available at http://lccn.loc.gov/2016003172

First Edition

Published in 2017 by
Gareth Stevens Publishing
111 East 14th Street, Suite 349
New York, NY 10003

Copyright © 2017 Gareth Stevens Publishing

Designer: Sarah Liddell
Editor: Therese Shea

Photo credits: Cover, p. 1 Eduard Kyslynskyy/Shutterstock.com; wood texture used throughout Imageman/Shutterstock.com; slash texture used throughout d1sk/Shutterstock.com; p. 5 Birdiegal/Shutterstock.com; p. 7 mlorenz/Shutterstock.com; p. 9 Steve Bower/Shutterstock.com; p. 11 Pictureguy/Shutterstock.com; p. 12 Wildnerdpix/Shutterstock.com; p. 13 TheGreenMan/Shutterstock.com; pp. 15, 17 Patrick Endres/Design Pics/First Light/Getty Images; p. 19 Denton Rumsey/Shutterstock.com; p. 21 Arnold John Labrentz/Shutterstock.com.

Printed in the United States of America

CPSIA compliance information: Batch #CS16GS: For further information contact Gareth Stevens, New York, New York at 1-800-542-2595.

CONTENTS

Words in the glossary appear in **bold** type the first time they are used in the text.

SO CUTE...
AND DEADLY!

Moose are the largest members of the deer family. They have a large **muzzle** and a mouth that turns up—almost like a smile. That's pretty cute, right?

Moose may look sweet, and just a bit silly, but don't get too close. These big **mammals** can be dangerous. In fact, more people are attacked each year by moose than by bears! Read on to find out why moose are so fearsome and how to know when a moose is about to strike.

THE DANGEROUS DETAILS
Moose have terrible eyesight, but excellent senses of smell and hearing.

ALWAYS EATING

Like other deer, moose don't eat meat. They like to chew on plants. They eat leaves, branches, and buds in spring. In winter, when few plants are growing, they eat bark off trees. Still, these plant eaters grow quite large. In fact, they're **massive**.

Moose are the tallest mammals in North America! Some grow to be as much as 7 feet (2.1 m) tall at the shoulder. They can weigh more than 1,300 pounds (590 kg), too. Male moose usually weigh more than females.

THE DANGEROUS DETAILS
A moose eats up to 50 pounds (23 kg) of food a day!

THE WORD "MOOSE" IS
AN ALGONQUIN INDIAN WORD
FOR "TWIG EATER."

LOOKING FOR MOOSE

Moose like to live in cooler places. They're found in northern parts of North America, Europe, and Asia. They live in forests, which provide them with cover from predators. They also like to live near water, such as a lake, stream, or pond.

Moose don't like it when the weather gets too warm. When it gets hot, you might see a moose swimming. They also walk into water to eat **aquatic** plants. A moose can stay underwater for as long as 50 seconds!

THE DANGEROUS DETAILS

The farther south a moose lives, the smaller it may be! Some in Wyoming are "only" 700 pounds (318 kg).

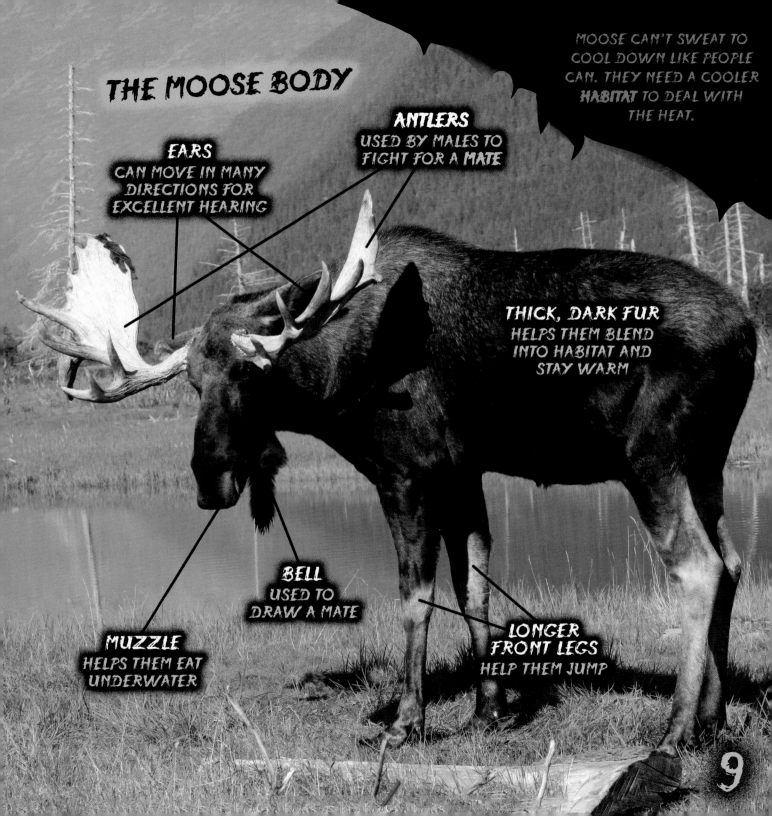

THE MOOSE BODY

EARS
CAN MOVE IN MANY DIRECTIONS FOR EXCELLENT HEARING

ANTLERS
USED BY MALES TO FIGHT FOR A **MATE**

MOOSE CAN'T SWEAT TO COOL DOWN LIKE PEOPLE CAN. THEY NEED A COOLER **HABITAT** TO DEAL WITH THE HEAT.

THICK, DARK FUR
HELPS THEM BLEND INTO HABITAT AND STAY WARM

BELL
USED TO DRAW A MATE

MUZZLE
HELPS THEM EAT UNDERWATER

LONGER FRONT LEGS
HELP THEM JUMP

WHAT MAKES A MOOSE MAD?

Moose like to be left alone to find food. They're usually peaceful. However, much like people, there are times when they're quite grumpy. For example, in winter, they're more **aggressive** than in summer. It's possible they're just hungrier and more tired from walking through deep snow in winter!

Unsurprisingly, moose are also aggressive when they feel threatened. Their enemies include animals that hunt and eat them, including bears, wolves, cougars, and people. Sometimes their enemies include other moose, too.

MOOSE CAN RUN
35 MILES (56 KM) PER HOUR.
THAT'S PRETTY FAST FOR SUCH
A LARGE CREATURE!

ARMED WITH ANTLERS

Male moose, called bulls, grow massive antlers. Antlers can be as wide as 6 feet (1.8 m)! They're used for fighting other bulls during mating season, usually September and October. Bulls fight each other for a mate. A moose may get more than 50 antler wounds every season from fighting. However, they have thick skin on their neck and front to protect, or guard, them.

After mating season, bulls lose their antlers and grow new ones for the next year. The special antler "skin" called velvet helps the antlers grow.

VELVET

THE DANGEROUS DETAILS

Rutting moose may
charge at cars!

MAD MAMA MOOSE

Female moose, called cows, give birth to one or two babies called calves in early spring. A calf stays with its mother for about a year.

Mother moose are fearsome when protecting their calves from predators such as wolves and bears. A mother might charge at these creatures and kick with her hard hoofs. A moose kick can easily kill a wolf. Still, about one-half of all moose calves die from predator attacks in the first 6 weeks of their life.

THE DANGEROUS DETAILS

A moose calf can outrun a person by the time it's 5 days old!

NEVER GET TOO CLOSE TO
A BABY MOOSE. ITS MOTHER
WON'T LIKE THAT!

15

THE MOOSE FIGHTS BACK

Moose have different ways of fighting back depending on the time of year. In winter, moose choose to take on wolf packs in places where the snow has blown away. This is so their legs are free to kick at their enemies. If they're stuck in deep snow, they back against thick evergreen trees to protect their rear legs from wolf bites.

In summer, moose fight wolves in shallow water. The moose can still kick, but the wolves can't move as well in water.

THE DANGEROUS DETAILS

After knocking down an enemy, a moose may try to **stomp** on it!

WOLVES ARE A
DANGEROUS ENEMY BECAUSE
THEY FIGHT IN PACKS.

17

WARNING SIGNS

If a moose is upset, it may show you in a few ways. Moose have a hump on their shoulders. When a moose is feeling aggressive, the hairs on the hump raise up. It may put its ears back and lick its lips, too!

These signs mean a moose may charge. Some charge a short distance as a warning. Even this is dangerous, as a bull moose may kick with its front hoofs when it charges. A moose won't usually chase someone far, though.

THE DANGEROUS DETAILS
Moose think dogs are a threat like wolves. They may kick them!

18

NOTICE THIS MOOSE'S HUMP HAIR IS STICKING UP. IT'S A GOOD IDEA TO GET BEHIND A TREE, FENCE, OR BUILDING IF A MOOSE IS WALKING TOWARD YOU!

THE MAGNIFICENT MOOSE

Moose face their greatest danger from people. They're an important source of food in Alaska. However, they're also threatened by people who think they're helping them. Some people feed moose. This makes moose expect people to feed them, and moose sometimes become aggressive with people who don't have food. Moose who attack people are killed.

It's best to leave moose alone in their habitat. As with most wild animals, moose are peaceful when left to themselves.

MOOSE MAY LIVE 15 TO 20 YEARS IN THE WILD IF THEY SURVIVE THE DANGERS OF NATURE—AND PEOPLE!

THE DANGEROUS DETAILS

According to the Alaska Department of Fishing and Game, hundreds of moose are killed each year when they're hit by cars. And sometimes the people in the cars are killed as well.

21

GLOSSARY

aggressive: showing a readiness to attack

antler: a bony, branched growth on the head of an animal

aquatic: living, growing, or spending time in water

habitat: the natural place where an animal or plant lives

mammal: a warm-blooded animal that has a backbone and hair, breathes air, and feeds milk to its young

massive: larger than what is usual

mate: one of two animals that come together to produce babies. Also, to come together to produce babies.

muzzle: the snout of an animal, consisting of the jaws and nose

stomp: to bring a foot down heavily in order to hurt something or someone

threatened: in danger

FOR MORE INFORMATION

BOOKS

Gish, Melissa. *Moose*. Mankato, MN: Creative Paperbacks, 2011.

Winnick, Nick. *Moose*. New York, NY: AV2, 2011.

WEBSITES

Moose
animals.nationalgeographic.com/animals/mammals/moose/
Find a map of the moose habitat and photos on this site.

Moose
www.adfg.alaska.gov/index.cfm?adfg=moose.main
Learn much more about the moose, and see video of it in action.

Moose: Facts About the Largest Deer
www.livescience.com/27408-moose.html
Read about the moose's special stomach on this interesting page.

INDEX